SchoolKidsLawyer's Step-By-Step Guide to IEPs

FOR TEACHERS

BY

ROBERT C. THURSTON, ESQ.

This book is dedicated to all children with disabilities and their families who don't know their legal rights in special education and to the good teachers out there who want to help.

I also dedicate this book to my love Michelle who inspires me every day to do better.

Published by Amazin Blue Press LLC.
© 2020 Robert C Thurston.
All rights reserved.

ISBN: 978-1-67813-944-5

TABLE OF CONTENTS

PREFACE

First thing: YOU CAN DO THIS!

We know that as a teacher, you have your students' best interests at heart. We also know that sometimes you face challenges from administration getting your students the help they need.

Second thing: TAKE A DEEP BREATH!

Knowledge of the laws on the IEP process will help you face those challenges head on.

We created this booklet to assist you in the IEP development process armed with knowledge of the law to help your students.

© 2008-present by Jess and Diary of a Mom.
© Copyright 2013 someecards, Inc.

IEPs: AN INTRODUCTION

An IEP is probably the most important document for a student with a disability's special education.

The main law to protect children with disabilities is the **Individuals with Disabilities Education Act**[1].

IDEA

All of what you will learn in this booklet is based on IDEA law and the legal rights guaranteed to the student and his/her parents.

If you're new to the world of special education, the first thing you should know is that if the student has a disability and is between the ages of 3-21, the public school owes the student a **Free Appropriate Public Education.**[2]

FAPE

You probably also keep hearing this term "IEP" and wonder what it is and if the student should have one.

---

[1] 20 U.S.C. §1400 *et seq.* Citations in this book will be to IDEA's code sections or IDEA's regulations, which are located at 34 CFR §300.1 *et seq.*
[2] 20 U.S.C. §§1412(a)(1) and 1413(a).

IEP stands for **Individualized Education Program** and if the student is eligible, the school <u>must</u> provide one. An IEP is a contract between the student's school, the child, and the child's family that describes how the school will provide the student with a FAPE through special education and services.

<u>Remember: FAPE is required and the goal of the IEP!</u>

WHAT IS AN IEP?

Let's start with a definition.

IEP Defined

In IDEA, IEP is defined as follows:

The term "individualized education program" or "IEP" means a written statement for each child with a disability that is developed, reviewed, and revised in accordance with the law.[3]

> Some people think that IEP stands for Individualized Education Plan. This is incorrect. An IEP truly is a Program because a plan implies a short term solution, whereas a program is a system for addressing all aspects of the disability in the school environment. It is much simpler to say "IEP".

Let's break down this into its three parts:

- Individualized: The challenge in special education is getting everyone to remember that the "I" in IEP means **individualized**. This means that the IEP must be designed with your specific student in mind. An IEP is not a generalized special education program

---

[3] 20 USC §1401(14); *see also* 20 USC §1414(d) and 34 CFR §300.320 *et seq.*

for all students with disabilities, but rather one that addresses the child's unique needs.[4]

- Education: The goal of an IEP is to ensure that each special needs child ultimately gets an education that enables independence and employment as an adult.

- Program: Special education is not simply a class that a student with a disability attends. Rather, it is a program that addresses **all** of your student's needs, including not only curriculum but also services, therapies, accommodations, devices, technologies, transportation, and other items used to help the student reach his/her specific goals.

> *Sometimes it is useful during an IEP meeting to remind the IEP Team that the "I" in "IEP" means "individualized" and that the focus must be on the needs of one specific child, not a general special education program. For example, if the student needs a private room to take tests, the IEP should be designed to meet that individual need.*

Don't overlook the portion of the definition which says it must be a <u>written statement</u>. Your

---

[4] The term "individualized" is used 10 times in 20 USC §1414. *See also* OSEP Letter to Clarke, March 8, 2007.

slogan should be: DOCUMENT EVERYTHING and WRITE DOWN EVERYTHING. Because . . .

IF IT AIN'T IN WRITING, IT DIDN'T HAPPEN!

So make sure everything is in writing – emails, letters, draft IEPs and proposed IEPs, descriptions of services, what the IEP Team says it will do . . . etc. EVERYTHING!

How does the student get an IEP?

The student needs to be determined "eligible" for an IEP under the law. To be eligible, the student has been declared a "child with a disability" and has educational needs that must be addressed. "A team of qualified professionals and the parent(s) of the student" shall determine if the student is eligible for special education services, thereby prompting the need for an IEP.[5]

IDEA defines a "child with a disability" as a child with:

- mental retardation (MR) / intellectual disability (ID);
- hearing impairments (including deafness);
- speech or language impairments (S/L);

---

[5] 20 USC §1414(b)(4); 34 CFR §300.306.

- visual impairments (including blindness);
- serious emotional disturbance (ED);
- orthopedic impairments;
- autism;
- traumatic brain injury (TBI);
- other health impairments (OHI); or
- specific learning disabilities (SLD)

and who, because of that disability, needs special education and related services.[6] The "<u>and</u>" part is very important as it makes the definition a **two-step analysis**; (1) the diagnosis; and (2) the need for special education and related services. If the student needs only a related service and not special education, the student does not qualify under this definition as having a disability.[7]

Many parents forget the second part of the IDEA definition - the need for special education and related services - and believe that the diagnosis is enough. It isn't. However, even if testing shows the student doesn't need special education and services academically, the need for special education and services is not purely an academic need; it is also functional behavior / social skills needs.[8]

---

[6] 20 USC §1401(3)(A); 34 CFR §300.8(a)(1).

[7] 34 CFR §300.8(a)(2). However, if the student has a disability but does not need special education services, the student may still qualify for protections under §504 or the ADA.

[8] *See* OSEP Letter to Clarke, March 8, 2007.

But, an IEP doesn't exist without an IEP meeting, which is a gathering of the IEP Team.

3 Quick Points

1. An IEP must be <u>individualized</u> and a <u>program</u> of special education and services designed to help the student with a disability.

2. The student must be deemed <u>eligible</u> by the IEP Team by having a <u>diagnosis</u> of a disability that fits into one of thirteen (13) categories **plus** <u>needs special education and related services</u>.

3. An IEP is a <u>written agreement</u> developed an IEP meeting by the IEP Team, so everything should be documented in writing.

THE IEP MEETING

Nothing happens in special education for the student until an IEP meeting takes place. Often IEP meetings can be confusing, disconcerting, overwhelming, stressful, and lots of other negative things.

But they can also be very positive events. The key to remember is that the goal is to help the student succeed. Preparation will conquer your fears and anxiety.

Who, What, When and Where?

While IEP meetings may be the most critical component of IEPs, there is no single law or rule that discusses these meetings. Rather, it is a series of separate references in the law which establish the rules of an IEP meeting. An IEP meeting should be scheduled far enough in advance so an appropriate IEP can be in effect for the next school year.

When must an IEP be in place?

An IEP must be in effect for each child with a disability at the <u>beginning of each school year</u>.[9] Schools must act promptly to put an initial IEP in place after determination of eligibility.

---

[9] 20 USC §1414(d)(2)(A); 34 CFR §300.323(a).

 After a school determines that the student is eligible, it must hold an initial IEP meeting and develop an IEP **within 30 days**.[10]

Most IEP meetings take place in the early Spring (approximately March) so that the IEP is in effect for the next school year. Another reason for the Spring meeting is to plan and make resources available for summer services (ESY[11]) and transportation.[12]

When must an IEP be reviewed?

In addition, the student's IEP shall be reviewed periodically, "not less frequently than annually."[13]

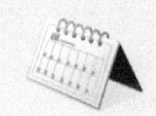 An IEP must be reviewed **at least once a year**. If the IEP is inappropriate for the student, it must corrected **immediately**.

But a parent or any other member of the IEP Team does not have to wait for the annual review to have an IEP meeting.

---

[10] 34 CFR §300.323(c)(1).
[11] ESY = "Extended School Year" services. 34 CFR §300.106.
[12] Transportation is a related service. 34 CFR §300.34.
[13] 20 USC §1414(d)(4)(A)(i); 34 CFR §300.324(b)(1)(i).

Who can request an IEP meeting?

Any member of the IEP Team may request an IEP meeting. A regular education teacher of the student, a special education teacher or special education service provider of the student, or the representative of the school district (LEA) are all members of the IEP Team.[14] A parent may also request an IEP meeting and their request may not be denied.[15]

You may request an IEP meeting at <u>any</u> time of the year and multiple times if necessary.

How do I know when an IEP meeting is scheduled?

When an IEP meeting is scheduled, the school will send out a Notice of the meeting to all participants.[16] The Notice must include the location where the meeting will take place.[17]

Where is the IEP meeting held?

Usually, the IEP meeting will occur at the school where the student attends. If the student does not attend the public school in his/her district, then the location of the meeting can be a mutually convenient place.[18]

---

[14] 20 USC §1414(d)(1)(B); 34 CFR §300.321.
[15] 20 USC §1415(b)(1); 34 CFR §300.501.
[16] *See* 34 CFR §300.322(a).
[17] 34 CFR §300.322(b)(1)(i).

What if I can't attend the IEP meeting?

If you are a member of the IEP team and are unable to attend, you may be excused from the meeting if both the parent and the school consent and you provide your input into development of the IEP in writing.[19] Also, if the IEP meeting is not addressing areas / curriculum involving you, you may also be excused.[20]

Who should be at the IEP meeting?

This is discussed in the next section of this book.

---

[18] 34 CFR §300.322(a)(2).
[19] 20 USC §1414(d)(1)(C); 34 CFR §300.321(e).
[20] Same as fn. 19.

What happens at the IEP meeting?

Typically, a sign in sheet will be circulated and everyone will be asked to introduce themselves. Then everyone present will have an opportunity to discuss the student's strengths and weaknesses in the school environment to determine what should go in the IEP. This is your time to tell the people assembled everything about the student.

BE HONEST. This is not the time to withhold information about the student – especially weaknesses – because it will only prevent an appropriate IEP. The administrators of the school should not interfere with your desire to help the student.

What should I do to prepare for the IEP meeting?

We have prepared a FREE guide called "5 Easy Steps for a Successful IEP meeting" to help you prepare.

 Download this FREE guide from our website at http://schoolkidslawyer.com/5-easy-steps-fo-a-successful-iep-meeting/

Can the parent audio or video record the IEP meeting?

Maybe. A frequent question from parents and advocates is whether they can audio or video record an IEP meeting about the student. Unfortunately, this is one of those questions for which the answer may be different from school district to school district.

The U.S. Department of Education (USDOE) Office of Special Education Programs (OSEP) issued a policy letter opinion on this subject and has said that it is a local policy issue and depends on several factors.[21]

There is no federal law allowing or prohibiting audio recording of IEP meetings. IDEA does not address it, nor do any of the other special education statutes. Audio recording an IEP meeting, when the IEP Team is aware and consents to it, is not a violation of federal privacy law. It is therefore left to the State Educational Agency (SEA) or local school district to determine the policy on tape recording these sessions.

---

[21] OSEP Letter Opinion, June 4, 2003 and Policy Memorandum 91-24, amending previous Policy Memorandum 88-17. These documents can be found in the Appendices of this Book.

See if your school district or the administration has a policy about audio recording of IEP meetings.

 Read our blog article on this topic at http://schoolkidslawyer.com/2017/11/22 /audio-recording-iep-meetings-is-it-allowed/

Development of the IEP

After these introductory steps, the real meat and potatoes of the IEP meeting begins. If a draft IEP has been distributed, the IEP Team will usually work from this document. If not, one of the school district representatives will take notes and collect reports for input into the IEP.

Draft IEP

Sometimes a draft IEP is distributed before the meeting to review and work from. Ask questions if necessary.

```
The US Department of Education frowns
upon distributing draft IEPs. However,
if your school district has prepared a
draft IEP, it should provide a copy of
the draft to all members of the IEP Team
prior to the IEP meeting.  The school
district may NOT have the final IEP
completed before the IEP meeting because
that is considered predetermination.[22]
```

How the IEP Team prepares the document

"In developing each student's IEP, the IEP Team shall consider:

- the strengths of the student;
- your concerns for enhancing the education of the student;
- the results of the initial evaluation or most recent evaluation of the student; and
- the academic, developmental, and functional needs of the student."[23]

The PLAAFP

Essentially, this is a discussion of the student's 'present levels of academic achievement and functional performance' or **PLAAFP**[24] and an explanation of the evaluations which will directly lead into the other parts of the IEP (annual goals, measurement, services, etc.).

Special Considerations

In developing an IEP, the IEP Team shall give special consideration in certain situations[25]:

---

[22] *See* Commentary, *Federal Register*, p. 46678.
[23] 20 USC §1414(d)(3)(A); 34 CFR §300.324(a)(1).
[24] 20 USC §1414(d)(1)(A)(i)(I); 34 CFR §300.
[25] 20 USC §1414(d)(3)(B); 34 CFR §300.324(a)(2).

- a disabled student's behavior that impedes his/her own learning or the learning of others;

- a student's limited proficiency in English;

- a disabled child who is blind or visually impaired;

- a disabled child who has communication challenges, such as being deaf or hard of hearing; and

- a disabled child who may need assistive technology devices and services.

Evaluations / Assessments / Testing

The IEP Team then goes through the evaluations, assessments, testing, and other data results (or updates). This is the time to have open and honest discussions about your student's disability and the challenges he/she faces in the education or social context. Sometimes these discussions are very difficult for a parent, but ultimately the IEP is helping the student through honesty. Just like a doctor can't resolve a stomachache unless the patient speaks up about it, no one can help the student with education or social skills unless those challenges are discussed - in other words, **ADVOCATE** for the student.

Goals and Services

Following these discussions, often the IEP Team members will offer proposals and recommendations for special education curriculum, services, teaching approaches, accommodations, and aids that are likely to assist the student to receive a FAPE. Your input is valuable here. Do not allow a school administration official deter your input.

> *If you have seen something succeed for the student, suggest the same technique for the IEP to build on that success.*

The Proposed IEP

After all of the components of the IEP have been discussed (*see* the last section to learn what is actually in the IEP) by the IEP Team, the designated scrivener or note-taker for the school district will create a proposed IEP or update the draft IEP. This proposed IEP must include <u>the date when services will begin</u>. Sometimes, the final draft won't be distributed during the IEP meeting – it may be sent later.

Parents <u>MUST</u> be given a copy of the final draft proposed IEP at no cost.[26] This is the law!

---

[26] 34 CFR §300.322(f).

Procedural Safeguards

The school district representative will typically take this opportunity to provide the parent(s) with a copy of the <u>Procedural Safeguards Notice</u>.[27] While the school district is not required to give this at the IEP meeting, they are required to make it available to the parent(s) at least once a year.[28] The annual IEP meeting may be the parents' only opportunity to receive this document.

A school district may also put a copy of the Procedural Safeguards Notice on its website.[29]

Signing the IEP

The school district must obtain the parent(s)' "informed consent" to provide special education and services for the student.[30] Consent is typically evidenced by a signature page at the end of the IEP, but may vary depending on whether it is the first IEP for the child or a subsequent IEP. In certain situations, consent rules are left to the states.[31]

If the parent doesn't agree with the proposed IEP, he/she may dispute it.

---

[27] 20 USC §1415(d); 34 CFR §300.504.
[28] *Id.*
[29] 20 USC §1415(d)(1)(B); 34 CFR §300.504(b).
[30] 20 USC §1414(a)(1)(D)(i)(II); 34 CFR §300.300(b)(1).
[31] 34 CFR §300.300(d)(2).

When all parties have signed the IEP, it is a contract for the educational placement of the disabled child with the goals and the specially designed instruction that will define the student's special education program and the school will proceed to implement it. That is the student's IEP until the IEP is next reviewed.

Prior Written Notice

Prior Written Notice (PWN) is required whenever the school district "proposes to initiate or change, or refuses to initiate or change the identification, evaluation, or educational placement of the student, or the provision of a free appropriate public education to the student."[32] In other words, if the school takes any action – refuses to issue an IEP; issues an IEP; changes placement – it must issue a PWN.

---

[32] 20 USC §1415(b)(3); 34 CFR §300.503(a).

3 Quick Points

1. The parent is the <u>most important participant</u> at the IEP meeting. You, as a teacher, must be prepared to honestly and fully discuss the student and how his/her <u>disability affects his/her education and social skills</u>.

2. The IEP meeting is where the <u>IEP Team</u> gathers to discuss the student's eligibility and needed <u>special education and services</u> to be <u>developed in an IEP</u>. <u>Advocate</u> for the student (even if the school administrators say not to).

3. The parent <u>doesn't have to sign</u> the IEP at the IEP meeting. The parent has the right to <u>dispute</u> the proposed IEP.

THE IEP TEAM

Your student's IEP will be developed by the IEP Team at an IEP meeting. If it's your first time attending an IEP meeting, you may be a bit surprised by the number of people in the room. So will be the parent(s). Luckily, you're reading this book. ☺

Mandatory Members

The IEP Team[33] consists of at least five (5) <u>required</u> persons. Those mandatory five members are:

(1)   The parent of the child with a disability;

(2)   Not less than 1 "regular" (general) education teacher of the student;

(3)   Not less than 1 special education teacher or provider of related services for the student;

(4)   A representative of the local school district with appropriate qualifications; and

(5)   Someone capable of interpreting the student's evaluation(s) results.

---

[33] 20 USC §1414(d)(1)(B); 34 CFR §300.321(a).

Ideally, each person on the IEP Team has specific knowledge of or experience with the student.

The Parent(s)

The parents of a child with a disability are mandatory members of the IEP Team. Indeed, "the concerns of the parents for enhancing the education of the student" is critical in developing the student's IEP.[34] Parental participation in an IEP meeting is so vital, it is set forth twice in the IDEA regulations.[35] IDEA's procedural safeguards guarantee a parent's opportunity to participate in the educational placement of the student.[36]

General Education Teacher

IDEA doesn't say much about the "regular" education teacher or what we call the general education teacher. The only language used is that such teacher should be on the IEP Team "if the student is, or may be, participating in the regular education environment."[37] What this means is that if the student is spending any time in the general education classroom, a teacher must be involved in the IEP process.

---

[34] 20 USC §1414(d)(3)(A)(ii); 34 CFR §300.324(a)(1)(ii).
[35] 34 CFR §§300.322(a), (c) and (d); 34 CFR §300.501(b)(1).
[36] 20 USC §1415(b)(1).
[37] 34 CFR §300.321(a)(2).

The GenEd teacher is a key person in the IEP meeting because he/she "shall, to the extent appropriate, participate in the development of the IEP of the student, including the determination of appropriate positive behavioral interventions and supports, and other strategies, and the determination of supplementary aids and services, program modifications, and support for school personnel."[38]

Special Education Teacher

The special education teacher or provider should be a person "responsible for implementing the IEP," so it might be a classroom teacher with a special education certification, the child's school speech pathologist, occupational therapist, physical therapist, one-on-one aide, or other person, depending on your student's disability and whether those services are in the IEP.[39]

School District Representative

The school district representative must be "qualified to provide, or supervise the provision of, specially designed instruction to meet the unique needs of children with disabilities; knowledgeable about the general curriculum; and knowledgeable about the availability of resources of the [school district]."[40] Typically,

---

[38] 20 USC §1414(d)(3)(C); 34 CFR §300.324(a)(3).
[39] *See* Commentary, *Federal Register*, p. 46675.

this individual is the Director of Special Education or a Superintendent for the school district.

Person to Interpret Evaluation Results

The school psychologist is almost always present as the one who can interpret the evaluation results. This is true even when that person is not the one who conducted the assessments or prepared the reports.

Optional Participants

Other <u>optional</u> members of the IEP Team[41] include:

    (1)   Other individuals who have knowledge or special expertise regarding the student

    (2)   When appropriate, the student

Other Individuals Selected by Parents

The "other individuals" provision is open to interpretation and may significantly increase the size of the IEP Team. The law reads: "at the discretion of you or the agency, other individuals who have knowledge or special expertise regarding the student, including related services

---

[40] 20 USC §1414(d)(1)(B)(iv); 34 CFR §300.321(a)(4).
[41] 20 USC §1414(d)(1)(B); 34 CFR §300.321(a).

personnel as appropriate."[42] This person may be a neighbor who knows the student very well (perhaps has babysat for the student); an educational expert who has observed the student in school or at home; one of the student's physicians; a person with an expertise in the child's diagnosis; and/or a special education advocate who can assist a parent at the IEP meeting.

> Although "advocates" are not specifically identified in IDEA, the "other individuals" designation in the IEP Team has created a cottage industry of parents of disabled children, paralegals, and other persons who are willing to act as the student's advocate on the IEP Team at IEP meetings. The only restriction is that "the determination of the knowledge or special expertise of any individual . . . must be made by the party (parents or public agency) who invited the individual to be a member of the IEP Team."[43]

Other Individuals Selected by School Districts

Such "other individuals" can also be identified by the school district. The school district may bring its own experts to the table – perhaps someone who has worked with the student, such as a

---

[42] 20 USC §1414(d)(1)(B)(vi); 34 CFR §300.321(a)(6).
[43] 34 CFR §300.321(c).

guidance counselor, lunch aide or playground supervisor.

The student?

IDEA says that "whenever appropriate, the child with a disability" can come to the IEP meeting.[44] But it does not explain what "whenever appropriate" means. That is usually left up to the parent. For transition planning, which usually occurs beginning when the student is 14 or older, the student <u>must</u> be present.[45] If the student is good at self-advocacy (speaking up about what is going on at school), then he/she may have some valuable input into the IEP. *A warning*: some things are discussed at IEP meetings that may be upsetting to the student. Consider whether the student should be excused for that portion or the entire IEP meeting for that reason.

> *Now you can see how the IEP Team may be much larger than five (5) people.*

---

[44] 20 USC §1414(d)(1)(B)(vii); 34 CFR §300.321(a)(7).
[45] 34 CFR §300.321(b)(1). This is for planning the student's future.

Special Issues

Can an IEP Team member be excused from the IEP meeting?

Members of the IEP Team may be excused from the IEP meeting or absent if their area of curriculum is not being modified or if the parent and the school district agree <u>in writing</u> that the member can submit his/her input to the IEP in writing.[46]

Can the parent be excused from the IEP meeting?

The school district has the responsibility to ensure that one or both parents are present at each IEP meeting.[47] This means giving proper notice sufficiently in advance to give the parent(s) a reasonable opportunity to attend and scheduling the meeting at a mutually agreed time and place.[48]

An IEP meeting may go forward without a parent attending, but only if such parent refuses to attend after proper notice and the school can't convince him/her/them otherwise.[49] The school district must keep adequate records of the attempts made to arrange a mutually agreed

---

[46] 20 USC §1414(d)(1)(C); 34 CFR §300.321(e).
[47] 34 CFR §300.322(a).
[48] 34 CFR §300.322(a)(1) and (2).
[49] 34 CFR §300.322(d).

time and place for the meeting, such as telephone calls, letters and visits to the child's home.[50]

Can the school's lawyer attend the IEP meeting?

Yes, but it is <u>strongly discouraged</u>.

OSEP addressed this issue in its 2001 policy letter.[51] While the "other individuals" provision in the list of possible IEP Team members theoretically includes lawyers representing either side and does not prohibit inviting attorneys to IEP meetings, OSEP quoted Congress to discourage such practice:

> The presence of an attorney could contribute to a potentially adversarial atmosphere at the meeting. The same is true with regard to the presence of an attorney accompanying [you] at the IEP meeting. Even if the attorney possessed knowledge or special expertise regarding [the student], an attorney's presence would have the potential for creating an adversarial atmosphere that would not

---

[50] *Id.*
[51] OSEP Letter Opinion, July 23, 2001, "Letter to Clinton".

necessarily be in the best interests of the student. <u>Therefore, the attendance of attorneys at IEP meetings should be strongly discouraged</u>.

3 Quick Points

1. The parents and you are <u>critical members of the IEP Team</u>. The school must make all efforts to schedule an <u>IEP meeting that is convenient</u> to the parents.

2. All <u>5 mandatory members</u> of the IEP Team <u>must be present</u> at an IEP meeting, unless they are <u>excused in writing</u>.

3. Both the parent(s) and the school may bring <u>additional participants</u> for the IEP Team if they have <u>special knowledge</u> about the student or your student's disability. The parent(s) may bring a <u>professional</u> who conducted <u>independent tests</u> of the student for their input into the IEP.

THE IEP

An IEP <u>must</u> contain the following:[52]

1. A statement of the student's present levels of academic achievement and functional performance (PLAAFP);

2. A statement of annual measurable goals;

3. A statement of how measurements of the student's progress towards those goals will be made;

4. A statement of special education and related services, and supplementary aids and services based on "peer reviewed research" that will be provided to the child and what modifications, accommodations, and school personnel will be provided to the child;

5. An explanation of the extent to which the child will not participate with non-disabled children in the "regular" (General Education) classes and activities;

6. A statement of any individual accommodations for taking or alternatives to the form of state or local standardized testing;

7. A statement on the projected date of when services and modifications will begin (when the

---

[52] 20 USC §1414(d)(1)(A); 34 CFR §300.320.

IEP will be implemented) and the frequency, location and duration of those services; and

8. When child is age 16+, a description of "transition services" to prepare the child for independent, adult living or, if not, what services the child will need as a disabled adult.

Nothing more is required in an IEP, but it must not be less than above. Additional information may be included if the IEP team believes it is necessary for the student's program.[53]

Key Elements of the IEP

The following is just a short description of these key elements of the IEP. A more in-depth discussion is contained in our book SchoolKidsLawyer's Step-By-Step Guide to Special Education Law.

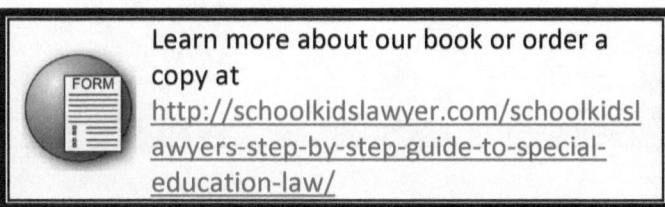

Learn more about our book or order a copy at http://schoolkidslawyer.com/schoolkidslawyers-step-by-step-guide-to-special-education-law/

PLAAFP

---

[53] 20 USC §1414(d)(1)(A)(ii); 34 CFR §300.320(d).

The law requires that the IEP include a statement of the student's "PLAAFP" [54] -

- Present
- Levels
- Academic Achievement
- Functional Performance

Academic achievement usually refers to how the child performs in the "core" subjects, namely reading, English (Literary Arts), math, science, and social studies.[55] Functional performance refers to non-academic skills such as social skills, participation in the classroom or activities, and behavior.[56] In other words, functional means how the child handles everyday life.

> The USDOE OSEP has declared in a Policy Guidance Letter that "the determination about whether a child is a child with a disability is not limited to information about the student's academic performance." Thus, the PLAAFP should not focus exclusively on the student's grades or tests in core subjects. Observations of behavior are also important.[57]

Goals

---

[54] 20 USC §1414(d)(1)(A)(i)(I); 34 CFR §300.320(a)(1).
[55] Commentary, *Federal Register*, p. 46678.
[56] Commentary, *Federal Register*, p. 46661.
[57] OSEP Letter to Clarke, March 8, 2007.

IDEA says that measurable annual goals should be designed to "meet the student's [academic and functional] needs that result from the student's disability" so that the child can make "progress in the general education curriculum" and to meet "other educational needs that result from the disability."[58] The goals must be measurable in order to track your student's progress.

Methods of Measuring Progress

The IEP must describe methods of measurement and "when periodic reports on the progress . . . will be provided."[59] Such measurements may be performed by testing, assessments, or other tools, but must be <u>reported to the parents</u> and those administering the IEP on <u>an agreed-to schedule</u>. This should be outlined in detail in the IEP.

---

[58] 20 USC §1414(d)(1)(A)(i)(II); 34 CFR §300.320(a)(2).
[59] 20 USC §1414(d)(1)(A)(i)(III); 34 CFR §300.320(a)(3).

Special Education and Services

After the goals and measurements are established, the IEP needs to describe what services will be provided to help the child reach those goals. The aids and services must be based on "peer-reviewed research to the extent practicable."[60]

This statement must describe the curriculum, related services, supplementary aids, modifications and the school personnel that will be provided to the child (1) to make progress towards the annual goals; (2) to make progress in the general education curriculum and participate in extracurricular and/or non-academic activities; and (3) to commingle with both disabled and nondisabled children in such activities.[61] Related services include if the student will have specialized transportation.

Extended School Year (ESY)

Another item that should be addressed is Extended School Year (ESY) services if the IEP Team determines such services are necessary to provide FAPE as part of the IEP development.[62]

---

[60] 20 USC §1414(d)(1)(A)(i)(IV); 34 CFR §300.320(a)(4).
[61] 20 USC §1414(d)(1)(A)(i)(IV); 34 CFR §300.320(a)(4).
[62] 34 CFR §300.106.

What is ESY? Download FREE materials about ESY on our website at: http://schoolkidslawyer.com/fskn-presentation-esy-and-comp-ed-february-24-2018/

ESY means "special education and related services that are provided to a child with a disability beyond the normal school year of the public agency; in accordance with the student's IEP; at no cost to the parents of the child; and meet the standards of the SEA."[63] In providing ESY, a school district may not limit ESY services to particular categories of disability or unilaterally limit the type, amount, or duration of those services.[64]

Typically, ESY is only available to students who may regress during the extended breaks (like summer) or have great difficulty recouping at the beginning of the next school year (or resumption of school, such as after winter break).

Placement

The law requires that children with disabilities be placed in the "least restrictive environment (LRE)." LRE requires: "to the maximum extent appropriate, children with disabilities . . . are

---

[63] 34 CFR §300.106(b).
[64] 34 CFR §300.106(a)(3).

educated with children who are not disabled, and special classes, separate schooling, or other removal of children with disabilities from the regular education environment occurs <u>only when</u> the nature or severity of the disability of a child is such that education in regular classes with the use of supplementary aids and services cannot be achieved satisfactorily."[65]

Stated more plainly, disabled children must be educated with non-disabled children to the greatest extent possible without interfering with anyone's education. The IEP must explain the amount of time and the reasons for which the student is removed from the general education classroom and where he or she will be during that time.[66]

Standardized Test Accommodations

In this section of the IEP, appropriate accommodations shall be listed that enable accurate measurement of a disabled student's performance on standardized assessments.[67] This may mean using a computer instead of a #2 pencil or taking the test in a quiet room.

---

[65] 20 USC §1412(a)(5); 34 CFR §300.114(a).
[66] 20 USC §1414(d)(1)(A)(i)(V); 34 CFR §300.320(a)(5).
[67] 20 USC §1414(d)(1)(A)(i)(VI); 34 CFR §300.320(a)(6).

Start Date

The implementation section of the IEP is not only to state when the special education and services will begin, but also how often, the location, and the length of time those services and modifications will occur.[68]

Transition Services / Planning

When the student reaches the age of 16 and for each year thereafter, this part of the IEP will contain a statement of "transition services." Put simply, the IEP Team is responsible for helping a child with a disability plan for the future.

Transition services are triggered by a student's 16th birthday. If this section is not filled in by the student's 16th birthday, an IEP meeting should be called to add it. Prior to the age of 16, this section will probably be blank.[69]

Implementing the IEP

Once the IEP is agreed to and signed, the school must then provide the special education and related services for the student on the date

---

[68] 20 USC §1414(d)(1)(A)(i)(VII); 34 CFR §300.320(a)(7).
[69] *See also* 20 USC §1414(d)(1)(A)(ii)(I); 34 CFR §300.320(d)(1).

indicated. The next question is when does the school have to start the services?

I've already stated that the school must have an IEP in place for each child with a disability at the beginning of the school year. But what happens if a child is found eligible during the school year?

 After the IEP team develops the initial IEP, special education and related services for that child must be made available **AS SOON AS POSSIBLE (ASAP)**.[70]

Availability and Distribution of the IEP

Best practices are to ensure each and every teacher and school staff member that may encounter the student has equal and full access to the student's IEP. Failure to do so might result in one teacher violating the IEP unknowingly or not knowing how to respond to a certain situation.

"Each public agency (school district) must ensure that the student's IEP is accessible to each regular education teacher, special education teacher, related service provider, and any other service provider who is responsible for its implementation."[71] In addition, each teacher

---

[70] 34 CFR §300.323(c)(2).

or provider should be informed of his/her respective, specific responsibilities to implement the IEP and what accommodations, modifications and supports must be provided to the student.[72]

> *Once the IEP is signed, best practice is to distribute a copy to every staff or administration person who might ever have any contact or interaction with the student.*

---

[71] 34 CFR §300.323(d)(1).
[72] 34 CFR §300.323(d)(2).

3 Quick Points

1. Be familiar with all of the <u>required sections</u> of an IEP and what they should contain, especially <u>goals</u>, <u>services</u>, <u>placement</u>, and the <u>start date</u> of the IEP. Make sure the goals and the student's progress are <u>measurable</u>.

2. If the student requires, make sure the IEP includes <u>ESY</u> and <u>specialized transportation</u>, in addition to the other listed special education and related services.

3. Remember: Because the IEP is a <u>written contract</u>, everything should be documented in writing. <u>If it ain't in writing, it didn't happen</u>.

To get more information on how your state handles special education and IEPs, go to this link: http://schoolkidslawyer.com/50-states-special-education-departments/

Other IEP Resources:

SchoolKidsLawyer's Step-By-Step Guide to Special Education Law

http://schoolkidslawyer.com/schoolkidslawyers-step-by-step-guide-to-special-education-law/

Wrightslaw.com: My colleague Pete Wright's excellent website on IEPs

https://www.wrightslaw.com/info/iep.index.htm

Understood.org: Great website on special education and IEPs

https://www.understood.org/en/school-learning/special-services/ieps

USDOE: A Guide to the Individualized Education Program

https://www2.ed.gov/parents/needs/speced/iepguide/index.html

NOTES